real, relatable
human moments

THE

MILLIONTH

MOMENT

KD GATES

At some point, you learn to love on those that love on you, and your world doesn't seem as dark anymore.

Contents

THE MILLIONTH TEAR

When I realized the millionth tear I cried would never empty the buckets of pain inside, I dried my tired, red eyes, changed my soaked pillowcase, and smiled as I bravely murmured, *"Healing happens now."*

As time goes on, life should grow and move with it. Yet, so many lay chained to internal pains, and rather than clinging to hope, they bond to hatred. Rather than living in the present moment, they unknowingly rest in the past.

Friends, I, too, was one of many resting in past moments, holding on to pain with great fears of letting go, only later to realize that somewhere between hurting and healing, I gained a desire for living, for breathing, and I've been inhaling and exhaling life ever since.

I want you to do the same; inhale hope, exhale possibility, and live.

MUCH LOVE.

MEMORY LANE

To the ones that felt pain,

love too, but mostly pain,

I see you.

As a girl,
I wore anger like the perfect black dress.
Not because happiness was wrinkled but
because black was both my wardrobe and
my feelings.

Can you relate?

Yet, my childhood was not all
bad, sad, thorns, and tears.
It was painful, but I am here,
stronger, wiser, and more powerful
than my past hoped I would be.

Not without the moments, though.

MOMENT #1

Little bastard child—
mortified mother,
knocked up; father in denial.
You little bastard, the love child.
No name to claim.
Father doesn't want you;
neither does shame.

Childhood rejection taught
me two things:

1. Some people create from pain.
2. Some people create from love.

MOMENT #2

Momma wanted me
and loved me
and healed me—
she created from love.

(L o v e)

MOMENT #3

I remember looking at Love and seeing the worry on her
face as she looked in the freezer to prepare dinner. And,
although she spoke no words, her anxiety did the talking.

Love feared failing at the job
she had been entrusted to do—
to be a good mother.

What Love did not know,
she was the best mother
a girl could ever have
raising a strong daughter
capable of the incapable
and courageous like the warrior.

I   a m   s h e .

Yet, while I was strong, capable,
and courageous, I was sometimes timid.
I found solace alone; it was my safe space,
at least until it wasn't.

(m o m e n t # 4)

Safety was not a gift for me;
it sometimes felt like a luxury
and heavier than I imagined.
The weight of degenerate
thinking and behaviors—
Pain and his snow (thin white lines),
Love and her kindness (my comfort space).

(m o m e n t   5)

MOMENT 6

There was no comfort
without forgiveness, though.
Love's pure heart always forgave
Pain's ungrateful one.

Cycle after cycle, it all repeats.

MOMENT #7

And repetition makes one realize
that sometimes Forgiveness and
Unconditional Love should never marry.

(t o x i c   l o v e)

The fear of loneliness
led to desperation,
which told determination that she couldn't
when she had all the power within
telling her that she could.

Yet, she didn't.

(L o v e)

MOMENT #9

In this life,
one must be braver than most
to conquer things meant to destroy them.
This includes people.

MOMENT #10

"You little bitch, you make me sick!"

I will never forget those words spewing from
Pain's mouth. He had been itching to say
them for years. And, while I am sure that I
provoked him, I am also convinced of this:

Sick people are sick and will never
know Sane.

(P a i n)

Yet, here I am—
here we are—
sanity intact—
survivors, realizing that moments
are meant to be shared.

After all,
books can't write moments.
Echo them, yes.
Write them, no.

Life does that.

If we have life and we are still not living,
then where is death?

(Life)

I came to understand that
breath, heartbeat, and brainwaves
are parts of life.

But living, seeking, and being emotionally,
spiritually, and vibrationally aligned
makes me whole, real, and alive.

So, it is okay to exist but,
it is far better to live.

After all,
life is an unwritten story,
a beautiful creation, aching,
longing to be read.

Yet, two questions remain:

1. Will you write your story?
2. Will you live it?

On this journey
I have learned that
bearing the unknown—
not dreading it—
makes living worthwhile
and living in the present moment even better.

Living presently helps us understand that
past pains have no place in the present.

Living presently allows us to release the
past and pay homage to the future.

Living presently
allows stillness and peace—
for us to just be,
while becoming
better versions of ourselves.

Leaving me to conclude
that living presently is not just any moment
but the moment of a lifetime.

A once-in-a-lifetime
chance to take the impossible
and achieve the extraordinary.

A chance to forgive
and a chance to seek forgiveness.
An opportunity to give thanks
and a time to be thankful.

A moment of peace
and a time of tranquility.

Because life,
sometimes hectic and chaotic,
makes all things possible.
Death is just an afterthought.

Today is a possibility.

(l i v e)

The rainbow hovers; the sun sits,

echoing the same question;

will earth ever heal?

Will humanity ever heal?

Will people change?

Can this world choose to
love too much and hate too little?

I believe it can.

It greeted me when I entered the world.
It was kind, gentle, and loving.
Never once did it tell me to live in fear.
Never once did it utter the words,
"freedom for others, not for you."

(h e r   b l a c k n e s s)

Never once did I hear
equality for them,
inequality for you.
I felt it, though.

(r a c i s m)

I spent years crying tears
for myself and other girls—
often questioning the whys and hows
of the world.

It was not until
I witnessed the battle between
good and evil,
pride and ego,
hope and hopelessness,
and realized that a massive part of the world
chooses evil and operates in ego.

So I weep.

I have wept for you
I still weep with you
but I smile and sing
and believe for you, too.

Do you believe in you?

And while this world is brutal,
look for the beauty amid the horrible,
peace amid the chaos,
warmth amid the cold,
solace amid the storm,
and find peace in possibility.

If we allow peace to become our reality,
perceiving peacefulness
as marvelous
rather than mania
makes life easier.
Much, much easier.

Gentle Reminder: A less complicated life
in this cruel world is never too much to ask.

The most influential parts of this world
are the connections we carry with us.
Wise connections produce greatness.
Foolish connections create fools.

This I believe.

(t r i b e)

I have learned that change
is like a chain reaction.
Links, good or bad, bind those connected to the chain
together. But one miserable link destroys a thousand good
ones. The world is no different.

(c o n n e c t i o n s)

Yet, there is still beauty in the world.

Find it, live it, share it, be it.

As you go forward,
take your power,
purpose,
and potential
with you.

As you go forward,
remember that a sapling oak takes
20 years to mature
and that life is no different—
wisdom, either.

Therefore, be patient with yourself;
maturity takes time.

NOTE TO SELF:

You are not fruitless.
Some fruit—
the sweet,
strong,
infinite kind—
takes longer to bloom.
Keep growing.

Strength is realizing
that the world will hold you in captivity
when it is not qualified to do so
and flying free anyway.

(s t a y   s t r o n g)

REMINDER

Every time you allow this world
to hold you captive, you minimize
your qualifications for freedom.

And a lack of freedom is the ultimate demise.

(d e a t h)

At some point, you have to choose life over the high. If you don't, you choose death, which, more often than not, is never the best choice.

Fate

Rejection,
is a form of fate,
a moment of death,
an art of being divinely protected.

And people will reject you
but never reject yourself—
your power lives there.

I remember praying for blessings—
yearning for answers and breakthroughs.
I never saw rejection as protection, a gift,
or a resolution until I saw rejection as
redirection and started traveling that way.

To truly be yourself, you must
be happy with yourself.

1. If you are not happy with yourself, you won't be happy with anyone else.

2. I have learned that rejecting the self is the highest form of neglect and the lowest form of self-respect.

3. Never forget that genuine happiness is not about someone else accepting you; it is about you learning to accept yourself even if no one else does.

(c o n t e n t m e n t)

REJECTION:

Too fat, ugly, skinny, tall, dark, light, rich, poor, imperfect, perfect. The word *"too"* will follow you, isolate you, and falsify your story. Find contentment in who you are and love that person.

After all, rejection should leave you wanting more of yourself. Allow that to be one of your greatest gifts.

She was never difficult to love;
her boundaries were difficult for others to accept.

REMEMBER:

Boundaries don't make you difficult to love;
they are difficult to accept by those not meant for you.

REPEAT AFTER ME:

Boundaries,
standards,
and expectations
are the backbones of
all healthy relationships.

Once you realize that rejection
kept you from the chaos
and brought you closer to calm,
you exhale, soar, and breathe through it all.

Make a commitment to yourself
to accept yourself for yourself.

Make a commitment to yourself
to accept the good, the bad, and the in-between.

Then, transform the internal,
and the external will always be beautiful.

Those are the highest forms of
self-acceptance.

Rejection can feel like
depression, an in-between, a maybe,
or a stark get lost at the cost of pain,
trauma, and heartbreak. But the heart still
beats, and if the heart still beats, it still loves.

She emptied her cup,
trying to nourish their soul,
only later to realize that selfish energies
are narcissistic energies
and narcissistic energies
are masters at rejection.

They will produce buckets of water
but would rather watch you dehydrate
before offering a glass.

(nourish yourself)

I removed myself
not because I thought I was better than you
but because I knew I deserved better.
And that, to me,
is always the best thing to do.

(h o w   i   n o u r i s h)

Staying in a place where
your heart and their heart no longer connect
is self-rejection, which is far more painful.

Rather, listen to the beat
and be aware of your heart's posture;
it will never reject you.

MY MOTTO:

Rejection may feel big,
but it's weightless compared to
acceptance, love, and surety.

Acceptance starts the moment
you accept yourself for yourself
without worrying if anyone else
accepts you.

Love is the catalyst to a life full of love.

Not a loveless life.

Insecurity is a deep, dark hole.

Surety is deep, but it is not dark.

We must look within
to find the root cause of our insecurity,
and deep digging is required.

Planting healthy seeds of surety
is optional but prosperous.

Insecurity is like an unwanted houseguest,
a shadow that only sees partiality
while consuming resources and
dimming your light.

Confidence entangles the whole spectrum.
When you capture the entire sphere,
you glow.

Glow like you are the world's only light source.

ENVY:

Is an internal massacre,
a bloody war between the heart and mind—
thoughts and reality.

(a form of insecurity)

Confidence is like fruit to a barren tree
still blooming in desolate soil.

SECURITY:

A sense of security is like fine linens—
the more comfortable you are, the better you feel.

Can you relate?

NOTE TO SELF:

Dummies fail to represent
who you are.
Always be yourself
and always define who you are—
authentically.

Fake is expected.
Real is rare.
Unique is best.

REPEAT AFTER ME:

I am a gift;
I will treat myself as such.

Unlearn the usual.
Once you do, you learn the extraordinary
and there is nothing ordinary about that.

There
is
nothing
ordinary
about
you.

It was an epiphany
when I realized the
best person I could be
was me, myself, and I.
It was like a shedding
of dead leaves for new ones
or a fertilization of something real—
like the uprooting of counterfeit
and the planting of authenticity.

I will grow here.

I cannot see you if I cannot see myself.
That is how self-confidence works.

That is how self-love works.

If we force-fake anything,
we begin misplacing our authenticity.
Sometimes for so long, we never find it.

The world does not
determine your acceptance.
The world waits for you to decide your
value, embrace your confidence,
and know your purpose.
It then treats you accordingly.

I do not long to be
something that I am not.
I long to be everything
that I know I am.
Without guilt.
Without shame.
Without fear.
Without doubt.
Without...

(s e c u r e)

RANDOM QUESTION:

If my "closest" friends love me,
why don't they support me?
I pondered that question so much
that I overlooked the friends that did.
And I thought, never again.
Never again will I take true love for granted.

DEEPER THOUGHT:

There's nothing more real than knowing
that while you're worried about falling,
people are watching,
praying,
and hoping
that you do.
Stop worrying.
Start doing miraculous things.

(i wonder)

I want to be so fearless.

I want to be so fearless
that when I lead, I will not
follow Fear because Coward calls out to me.
I will follow the echoes of Potential
and Confidence, and Faith instead.

Fear, life's natural necessity,
can also be life's immoral captivity.
It operates in void spaces and places.
Give it a cup, and undoubtedly,
it will overflow.

Fear is
one-eighth of life's cycle.
Do not let it become a whole.

(h a v e   c o u r a g e)

Regarding fear, I have learned two things:

1. It does not prevent failure.
2. It does bury success.

Don't let it bury you.

Fear is not survival.
Refrain from mixing the two.
Fear is unkempt and often disguises itself
as a well-meshed safety net.
Most likely, it is concealing your destiny
and drowning your dreams.
Do not be fooled.

(b e   v i c t o r i o u s)

We have all been there,
drowning beneath scared shadows
while muting our talents to please fear.
But, I have learned that paddling through fear
does not make us weak swimmers,
it makes us courageous captains.

(be fearless)

Obstacles come and go,
some bringing fear,
others bringing motivation.
Either way, we overcome.
Either way, we swim.
Either way, our boats don't sink.

DEAR FEAR:

Black clouds rested above my head
for so long I had forgotten the sky's
blue beauty. I began missing the sun's warmth
and the moonlight at midnight.

Finding comfort in the dark, I stopped seeking the light, and
rather than liberation, I lost my motivation and forgot to live.

Yet, Life remembered me.

Life reminded me that where there is darkness, there
is light; one must trust in Hope to take them there.

MUCH LOVE,

Me

REMINDER 1:

Healthy fear is a thing.

REMINDER 2:

Fear is enormous to Doubt
but little to Courage.

REMINDER 3:

Fear is the opposite of courage.
And if you can be fearful, you
can be courageous.

REMINDER 4:

Fear can be big
but good energy consumes it.

I travel forward
not because I fear what's behind me.
But because I'm excited to see
what's ahead of me.
My spirit tells me it's something
unfathomably GOOD.

Good energy echoes
the vibrational moment where fortification
meets determination, and we begin shedding
old interiors for new ones.

Echo

To connect with the internal divine,
we must unify with the Infinite Ultimate—
viable energy starts there.
Limitless energy lives there.

Energy is an incomparable love;
it is forever changing.
You can't ignore it.
You can't numb it.
You can't hide from it.
Sooner or later,
it consumes thoughts
and haunts dreams.
Embrace it gracefully.

Energy is life's misunderstood element.
Shareable, yet, often kept in left field
to charge alone.

(r u n n e r ,   c h a s e r)

Yet, energy is a solo vibe,
but it's better when shared.
So, when a person's energy can
penetrate you without consummation,
that is a soul you want to keep,
captivate, and marry.

(s o u l f o o d)

ENERGETIC ADJECTIVES:

1. euphoric
2. breathtaking
3. sensational
4. invigorating
5. electrifying
6. undeniable
7. unforgettable
8. incomparable
9. _____
10. _____

Energy is fluid, yes.
But it is a frequency,
a vibrational pull, an emotional,
and a spiritual experience, too.
Feel it.

(v i b e s)

Her love is climatic.

It is void of surface
and consists of countless levels—
energetic, deep, and often too deep
for the faint and weak.

Her energy is etheric.

Her aura speaks virtuous dialects
unknown to some. But to the one,
they will come, decipher them all—
translation is not needed.

(matriarch)

Energy is synergy—
the effects of what was,
what is, and what's to come.

Ground yourself.

Allow your energy
to represent the inner you—
the intertwining of ethereal
and divine forces.
Your well-being rests there.

·

There is a destination
in the energy that you carry.
Where it takes you depends
on your moral compass
and the distance you are willing to travel.

How far are you willing to go?

Most energy is subtle.
It can be magnetic and charismatic, too.

(v e l o c i t y)

The energy we keep
tells a compelling story.
Positive energy writes a positive script.
Negative energy writes a short novella.
Either way, our internal words
become our external story.

Either way, our external story
speak our internal words.

What story are you telling?

I felt that deeper than I wanted to.

(p a i n)

Before we can heal,
we must understand the cause
of our wounds.

Only then can we comprehend
and heal our pain.

Only then can two halves become whole.

While transmuting pain
is difficult, it is doable.
After all, there is no transformation
without difficulty, doubt, or defeat.

(s t a n d u p)

PAIN IS:

Pain is deep.
Pain is familiar.
Pain is inevitable.
Pain is not forever.

RELATABLE:

The moment when you pretended
to be okay in the light
yet felt lost in the dark.
That moment is familiar.

VERY RELATABLE:

That moment when you lied,
convincing yourself that the
pain you feel, you feel no more.
That moment is familiar, too.

The more
one holds on to painful experiences,
the more one holds on to a painful past—
the more one denies a beautiful future.

Painful experiences
are challenging to embrace.
But, once you accept the quest
and move past that, the pain becomes not just
an experience but a personal healing journey.

If you mute your pain,
your pain will mute you.

If you hide your pain,
your pain will hide you.

If you confuse your pain with pleasure,
you will confuse your pleasure with pain.

PRAYER:

In confusion,
I prayed for Clarity.
In the chaos,
I prayed for Calm,
In heartbreak,
I prayed for healing.

I've received them all.

CLARITY:

Allowing the flesh
to become intimate with confusion
is one of the worst sacrifices we can make—
and one of the most painful.

Love is the opposite of hate,
just as pleasure is the opposite of pain.
And one can only hate if one was
never taught to love.

PASSIVE-AGGRESSIVE

He gifted her beauty in a box.
Eagerly, she placed it against her skin.
Smiles surround her face and glistening eyes;
she felt alive.

He gifted her ego in a box,
and she placed it against her skin.
Ego whispered, "You are pretty,
but you'd be prettier if you were thin."

NARCISSIST

Picture it. You're trying on that dress, the one
you've wanted for quite some time. Surprise! He
gives it to you as a gift. He tells you how nice
it will look and convinces you to wear it.

You think, "Wow! He has finally done something
nice for a change. Maybe he does love me."

So, naturally, you find enough courage to try
on the dress, and once on, you are in awe of the
dress's look, fit, and appeal. You feel amazing!

Or at least you did until he looked at you and said,
"It's nice, but it would look nicer if you were thin."

His grin, your frown, as your heart stops, your
mouth drops, tears too because the man you
loved has become the abuser you hate.

QUESTIONS TO CONSIDER:

- Were you created to be abused?

- Would you treat yourself the way you

  allow others to treat you?

- Is this your meaning of love?

- Is staying worth it?

Love Is:

Love is patient and kind. Love does not envy or
boast; it is not arrogant or rude. It does not insist on
its own way; it is not irritable or resentful; it does
not rejoice at wrongdoing, but rejoices with truth.

(1 Corinthians 13:4-8)

Suffering in silence
because you fear provoking shame,
prolongs pain and increases shame.

(e m o t i o n a l   a b u s e)

Being silent
about your pain
does not make your
pain irrelevant or any less real.
And, just because your suffering was silent
does not mean your hell wasn't loud.

(s a y   s o m e t h i n g)

Actions and emotions speak.

It is a skill to listen.

Those courageous enough
to sit with their pain,
feel it, embrace it, release it, and heal it
are capable and brave enough to heal others.

I want to know those people.

Internal pain
is not eternal punishment,
making transmutation,
the process of turning your pain into power,
the ultimate celebration.

The prerequisite is to show up.

Once upon a time,
before healing,
I realized that pain was
the oppressor of happiness,
and happiness, if you can push through
the pain, was the successor of it.

So I decided to heal.

Because happiness,
like any other assignment,
must be the lesson to our pains in this life.

Yet, grief does happen.

GRIEF IS:

Grief is growth in disguise—
it hurts but your evolution is everlasting.

It only feels like forever.

(g r i e f)

Grief is suffering,
but it is not a permanent sacrifice.
It is temporary, and it, too, shall pass.

(p a t i e n c e)

As the tears swell in her eyes,
his too, grief so intense, will they survive?
Will he fold as he hides behind pride?
Wishing to release grief,
will they find peace?

(grief is neutral)

I pretended not to care to cope.

(a g o n y)

Heavy drops to the ground;
drowning hearts pound
the crying never stops
as life keeps moving,
racing against the clock
as she sits, he quits, and they resist the
inevitable gift called healing.

(d e s p a i r)

You will cry, and you will yearn.
You will fall, and you will get up.
But you will be okay.

REMINDER:

Grief is heaviest when we clinch the tightest.

(let go)

HOW TO HEAL GRIEF:

Feel it.
Embrace it.
Understand it.
Accept it.
Release it.
Breathe.

I won't tell you to breathe through it, but I will
encourage you to take deep breaths along the way.

Doing so aligns emotion and logic—
balance and rhythm.

Grief takes us to dark places
and void spaces, and mentally,
like savage animals, we fight.
It is the Spirit that guides us to the light
and our determination that allows us to fly.

(s o a r)

Grief, despair, and pain
are the mammoths of life.
Faith, hope, and strength are the warriors.

Let them win your war.

I have felt the depths of grief,
and I have felt the depths of healing.
Both have a purpose.

Grief was planted,
but it was love that blossomed.

Last night,
I went to bed as a child
and awoke as an adult, ready to live,
love, and hope again—
authentically this time

FracTion

Even fractured hearts
are capable of loving.

Love is the revolution,
not the war.

If love can move mountains,
can you imagine what true love can do?

It is not rare
to feel hurt before you feel hope.

It is rare
to feel hate before you feel love.

The heart seeks many wonders;
joy, peace, and healing.
Yet, gentleness is the one love
the heart yearns for,
skips a beat for,
and breaks.

REMINDER:

Sometimes love goes,
and sometimes love stays.

Society will tell you that falling out of love
meant you were never in love,
which is not true.

You can be in love,
be full of love,
and bleed love,
but the right love in the wrong place
becomes unbalanced love.

Can you relate?

Yet, lasting love often feels
unbalanced, fleeting, reckless, and greedy.
It is an intimate desire, a delectable delight,
a moment we secretly crave, hoping to
find a connection and a love that lasts.
Both appetizing and beautiful.

LOVE **VS.** LIKE

Love says, *"here is my heart."*

Like says, *"let me think about giving it to you."*

And, if they have to think about giving you their heart, let them keep it.

Their love was asphyxiation;
their presence was oxygen.

(o b s e s s i o n)

I've been here before.
Have you?

Your toxicity scares me,
but it intrigues me, too.

(l o v e - s i c k)

LOVE **VS.** LUST

Love is deep and looks beyond the exterior.
Love is about connection, not control.
Love is patient, kind, and caring.
Love is committed and long-lasting.

Lust is superficial and only sees the exterior.
Lust is about sex, not substance.
Lust is greedy, selfish, and needy.
Lust is temporary and short-lived.

Which would you prefer?

GRATITUDE:

Gratitude helps you understand
and fall in love with the real you:

The person who is grateful for being.
The person who is grateful for individuality.
The person who is grateful for the experience.

And, if you are grateful for those things,
you can't do anything but love who you are.

To love the self is to be kind to the self.

Self-love says the more we love ourselves,
the more we can love others.

Yet, to love ourselves, we must know ourselves.
Only then can we truly love and give love to another.

Love is a language,
and self-love is a dialect.
One of the most incredible talents in life
is knowing how to speak and understand
them both.

Cheating,
bleeding,
and adulterous hearts are a part of life.
They should not be a part of your love life.

Monogamy is a love language,
adultery is not.

I bring a lot to the table.
But if you're never full,
how can you ever be satisfied?

(w o m a n i z e r)

To desire another's heart
when you have their good heart
makes the grass seem greener
on the other side.

My promise to you;
the grass is just as brown.

(l u s t)

Fake fantasies
minimize good people
seeking real love.

My promise to you:
The fantasy is seldom true.

Live in the present moment.

It started.
It was fun.
It is over.
It is done.
A ~~love~~ story.

(friends with benefits)

HOW WILL I KNOW
MY SOULMATE:

Energy so intense it's vibrant.
You will not question leaving.
You will long to be present in their presence.
Leaving is never an afterthought.
Because the one meant to stay
will come and stay forever.

GHOSTING:

We may never know their why,
and we must be okay with that.

Ghosting, a trait of the weak.

Love is a profound thought
thinking in the present moment.
So, when they say you think too deeply,
tell them to find shallow
and then go and seek real love elsewhere.

I discovered one of many love lessons
when I concluded that heartbreak happens.
And pretending to love the heart
that broke my heart again
would be fooling myself—
AGAIN.

I also realized that sometimes,
it is their kiss that we miss.
Not them so much.

(r e m i n i s c i n g)

Often,
forgetting is the best medicine.

(h e a r t b r e a k)

Looking for love
in all the wrong places,
on all the false faces,
will leave you with an empty cup.

Two halves do not make a whole.
Two halves create more halves.
Wholeness starts within.
Allow it to fill your cup.

SAFE SPACE

The space felt safe until it became your pain.

Picture it; you have finally found the one, a safe
space, a lover, and a friend that listens, protects, and
cares. You feel so safe that you tell them your deepest
secrets, and because the solo weight you once carried
is no longer heavy, you breathe deep and release.

In essence, you feel like you've found freedom,
and the thought of fear no longer haunts you.

Untill one day, the person you thought you knew, kind,
loving, honest, and gentle, becomes cold, careless, and cruel.

The friend you thought you knew is now
an unrecognizable stranger.

The safe space you thought you had has now become
your pain. And the only thing left for you to do is cry.

And cry.
And cry some more
until you realize:

all the nights your tears
soaked the feathers in your pillow,
the birds cried,
you cried,
they never did.

(m a n i p u l a t i o n)

But be grateful for the tears
because the safe love you seek will
seek, honor, and keep you.

(h o l d   o n)

THE ONE:

1. Looks at you and sees you.
2. Believes in you.
3. Fears losing you.
4. Respects you.
5. Pushes you to be the best.
6. Does not compete with you.
7. Is honest with you.
8. Listens to you.
9. Forgives you when right to do so.
10. Loves you.

A hurting heart still beating
is a heart capable of healing—
a heart capable of loving again.

One of life's many goals is sharing your heart,
not giving it away or allowing it to stay
shattered when and if in pieces.

(b r o k e n   h e a r t)

In love,
your time is valuable.

Out of love,
your time is valuable.

Honoring your time
is a display of love.

Loving yourself
is one of the highest forms of self-love
and one of the most valuable
forms of self-respect.

ONCE YOU UNDERSTAND:

- That 'no' is a complete sentence.

- That not being available constantly is okay.

- That resting is rejuvenation.

- That you are worthy of peace.

- That genuine love is what you deserve.

- That rewarding yourself is a good deed.

You understand that self-love isn't selfish;
it's solace, an essential commitment to your
success, well-being, and happiness.

Dimming your light
for the one you love
causes you to get lost in the dark.
This is not an act of self-love.

(k e e p   s h i n i n g)

Selfish love is greedy.

Selfish love is inconsistent.

Selfish love does not fill voids;

it creates them.

Genuine love is generous.
Genuine love is meaningful.
Genuine love is lasting love.

Some love is terminal.
Some love is infinite.

Giving your heart to the One
is risky.

Giving it to yourself first
is a guarantee.

When you love yourself first,
you understand what genuine love
feels and looks like.
And anything other than that,
you're not willing to tolerate.

(n e v e r s e t t l e f o r l e s s)

Never wilt for love.

A love that causes wilting is a dying love.

A love that pushes you to bloom
is a living love.

SEEDLING

Love is a seed.
Plant it.
Water it.
Feed it.
And watch it grow.

EVERLASTING LOVE

The breakdown
and the rebuild are fortifying.
And both open the door
to everlasting love,
newfound strength,
and the ability to heal
and hope
and live.
Again.

Be open to the process.

I am loveable.

I am loveable.

I am loveable.

REPEAT AFTER ME:

I am loveable.
I am loveable and I am seen.
I am loveable and I am wise.
I am loveable and I am heard.
I am loveable and I am joyful.
I am loveable and I am enough.
I am loveable and I am blessed.
I am loveable and I am grateful.
I am loveable and I am confident.
I am loveable and I am hopeful.

BECOMING:

We become what we repeat.
We become what we don't repair.
Tell yourself good things.

HopE:

Hope must be the gateway to healing
because if I can't hope and believe in what
I am hoping for, healing is far from me.

I remember when I was a little girl,
hoping and wishing for a new reality.
Hope never came.

The older I got, I stopped looking.
The more centered I became, Hope came.

(i am hopeful)

Find your center, and hope will find you.

If you can't see in the dark,
trust in hope to find the light.

If problems exist,
so do possibility and hope.
Hope is one of the many possibilities of life.

FAILURE VS. HOPE

Failure gives us rendezvous and multiple
chances to play with it.

Hope gives us commitments,
signed contracts, and real availability.

Failure is brute.
Hope is honest.

Once you have met the two,
you will never entertain failure again.

(s u c c e s s   w a i t s   f o r   y o u)

Hope is the missing piece
that causes you to collide with purpose,
make an impact on vision,
and courageously shatter success.
And, once you find hope,
there's a high chance of you
finding success, too.
Stay determined.

Look at the image
and tell me what you see.

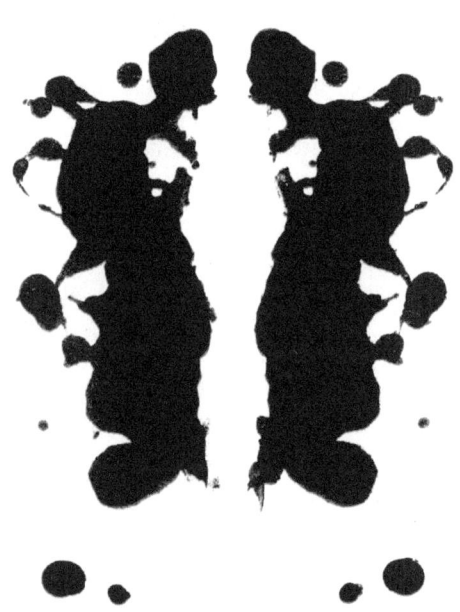

If you saw a reflection of excellence,
your potential, and your purpose,
you are off to a fantastic start.

Get started.

SOMETIMES,
HOPELESS FEELS LIKE:

- Things are not getting better.

- I have tried that already.

- This will never change.

- Every step that I take, I fall further behind.

- I cannot do this.

- When will I win?

- Will this ever end?

SOMETIMES,
HOPEFUL FEELS LIKE:

- Things are getting better.

- I tried before; I will try again.

- Things will change.

- Every step is a good step.

- I can and I will.

- I am a winner.

- This pain will end soon.

When I hope,
I can exhale.
And when I exhale,
I can breathe—
freely.

When I hope,
I can dream.
And when I believe,
I can achieve—
great things.

Hope through the heavy,
healing lives there.

(r e l e a s e)

HEALING:

Healing and pain
make up life's spectrum.
Healing never opposes pain,
and pain never refuses healing.
Without one another, neither would exist.

Without one another,
growth, breakthrough, and
evolution would not exist.

Healing is not
the chaser or the opponent of light.
We are the runners and the antagonizers.
Scared and afraid of the unknowns and
uncertainties the light will bring.

If I pretended healing was easy,
I would be lying.

Healing has to fight the good fight
of being outnumbered.
It has to battle the ego, pride,
and trivial opinions of its host.

I'm not saying it's a wish list to heal.
But it sure is discipline on the
backbones of determination

(y e a r n & f i g h t t o h e a l)

Healing is alignment in motion—
it captivates the entire being.
Where it goes, I follow.

MIND + SOUL + SPIRIT

Mind, soul, and spirit perfectly align when
they enter the state of whole healing.

Yes, thoughts of revenge will come,
but in the end, Healing says to let go,
and your submissiveness says to follow.

That is the true nature of a spiritually
and emotionally healed person.

(a l i g n m e n t)

SELF + HEALING

Self-healing is the craving for wholeness.
It's the process of healing yourself
emotionally, spiritually, and mentally.
Definitely a full-circle moment.

SELF-DEPRIVATION:

Her need to be needed was vast;
she gave herself to anyone: the abuser, the
liar, the two-faced friends for hire.

SELF-HEALING:

Her need to be needed was non-existent
because her need for *herself* was enough.

MISTAKES:

Mistakes lead to hurting,
but I see mistakes as healing moments in disguise.

Mistakes are opportunities to understand that while they
come, knock us down, and cover us in the dirt, forgiveness,
the successor of mistake, shows up and gives us love.

And love, like forgiveness, is the ultimate blessing.

HOW TO HEAL PART I:

Cry. Laugh. Cry some more.
Feel and embrace.
Surrender and express your pain.
Respect the silence.

HOW TO HEAL PART II:

Accept and understand that
choosing to heal is an act of self-love.
Breathe deep, inhale, exhale, and release.

HOW TO HEAL PART III:

Find faith, make peace, and just be
while remembering that life moves on with
or without us and that choosing to stay stuck
in grief, pain, or darkness is a choice.

Dark souls
yearn for healing
by hurting the healed.

Light souls
understand that hurting others
is something hurt people do
and that karma, on the other hand,
is something fate does.

When we dedicate a part of our lives to healing
and releasing wounds, our will to remove
doubts and fears becomes our reality.

Our pain is different;
our reactions are different.
But pain impacts us the same.
It leads us down the familiar yet
mental road of having therapy sessions
with Cope and Overcome.

Eventually, we must ask ourselves:

Will we *just* cope?
Or, will we overcome?

Recovery is the road less traveled,
but it is still a road.

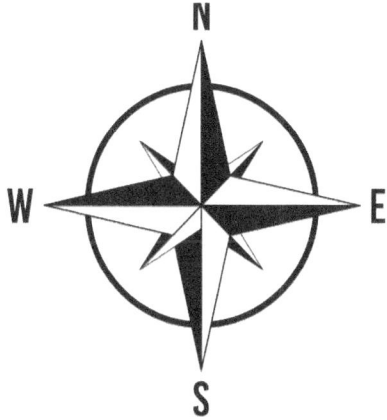

Pick a destination and go that way.

Healing waits in unlikely places.

During childhood,
I experienced hurting before healing.

During adulthood,
I abandoned healing because the hurt
became familiar, and the emotional injuries
became my power.

Yet, the mind is intricate and far more powerful,
gripping memories and believing reality.

Like the alterations of a designer dress,
the flexibility of the mind is a delicate fabric,
obeying our every command.

If we stitch hurt, hurt stays.
If we mend healing, healing comes forth.

What have you
sewn lately?

There was a point in my life
where I told my hurt child goodbye
and the healed adult hello.

Indeed, healing and transformation
can only occur when we make it to that point.

As an adult,
I wear joy like the perfect white shirt.
Not because anger is wrinkled
but because
hope is pretty,
peace is purpose,
happiness is a classic,
and laughter is the new black.

(the perfect outfit)

Find a mental wardrobe
that is daring enough to say;
I am healed and bold enough to believe it
this time.

When you heal,
you have an opportunity to believe
"every good thing follows me"
and a greater opportunity to
act upon that belief.

Every
good thing
follows me.

Embrace the painful side of healing;
your breakthrough waits on the other side.

(b r e a k t h r o u g h)

On the other side of healing
lives a celebration of moments.
Don't forget to cheer for yourself.

In the meantime,
understand that hurting happens,
but so does healing.

Hurting brings Chaos,
and Healing brings Calm.

While they both have the potential
to bring Growth, *only* Healing can bring Peace.

That I know for sure.

T

MILL

MON

E

ONTH

ENT

To the soul that found me—
thank you for *sharing* this moment.

DEAR FRIEND,

The Millionth Moment shares fractions of
relatable moments, some that I have lived
and those that are yet to come.

And, like me, you, too,
will have millions of moments.

Take joy in them, be present, and don't hesitate
to celebrate them all—the good, bad, sad, and
in-between moments.

Your happiness waits there.

MUCH LOVE,

KD Gates

1 2 3 4 5 27 26 25 24 23

ISBN: 979-8-9852433-8-3

Library of Congress Control Number:
2023939512

Editorial design and direction by:
The Story Laboratory

Cover design by:
Ebook Launch

Visit kdgates.com to learn more.

www.ingramcontent.com/pod-product-compliance
Lightning Source LLC
Chambersburg PA
CBHW020227130626

46549CB00005B/1776